PRESENTED TO

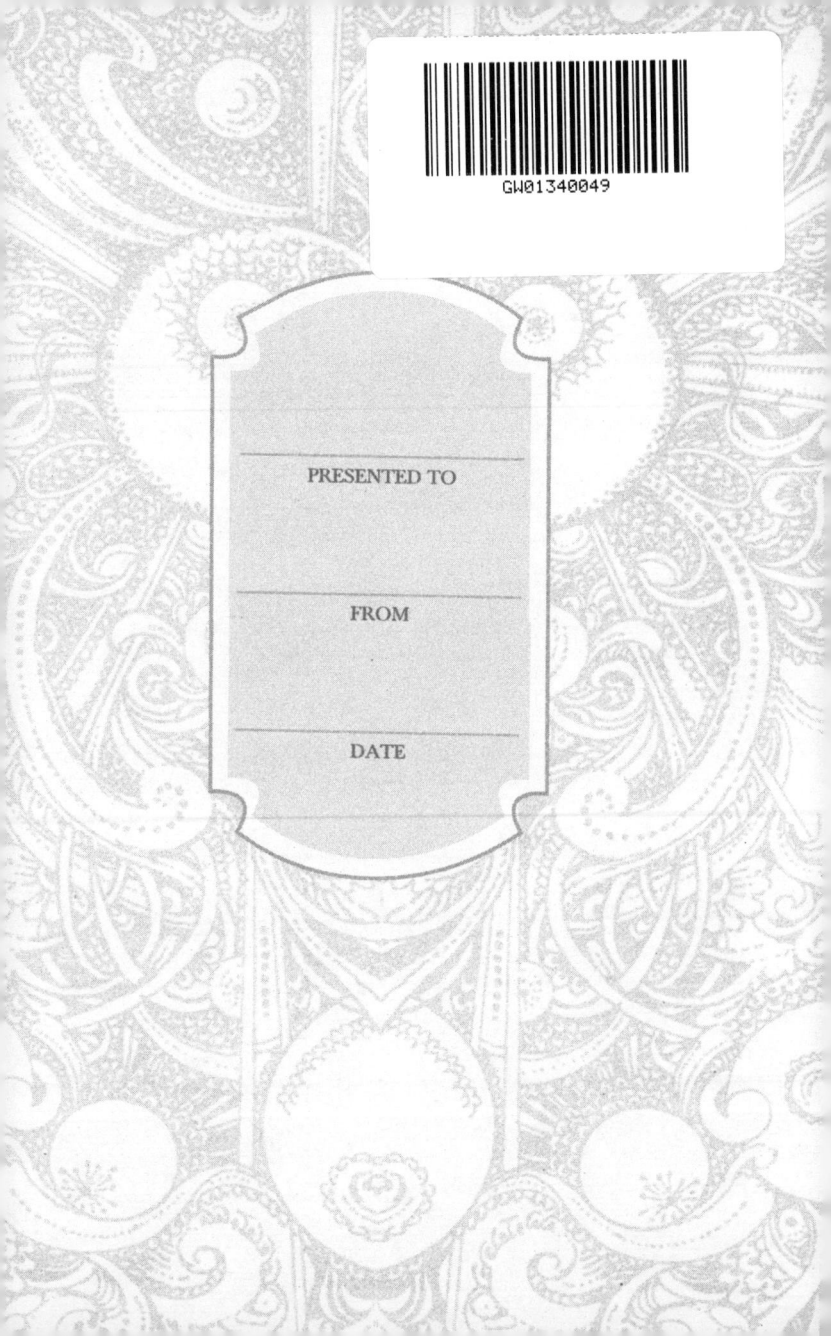

FROM

DATE

Inspiring Thoughts

₹ 150

ISBN : 9788170286844

Edition : 2015 © APJ Abdul Kalam

INSPIRING THOUGHTS by APJ Abdul Kalam
Printed at Deepika Enterprises, Delhi

RAJPAL & SONS

1590, Madarsa Road, Kashmere Gate, Delhi-110006
Phone : 011-23869812, 23865483, Fax : 011-23867791
website : www.rajpalpublishing.com
e-mail : sales@rajpalpublishing.com

Inspiring Thoughts

APJ ABDUL KALAM

rajpal

What would you like to be remembered for? You have to evolve yourself and shape your life. You should write it on a page and that maybe a very important page in the book of human history

Encourage all children to dream for themselves. Unless they have dreams they will not be motivated to attain them

The 'dream-thought-action'
philosophy is what
I would like to be inculcated
in each and every student

Creativity is seeing the same thing as everybody else, but thinking of out-of-the-box solutions

Quality leaders are like magnets, they attract the best people

𝒞reative leadership is
exercising the task to change
the traditional role
from commander to coach,
from manager to mentor,
from director to delegator and
from one who demands
respect to one who facilitates
self-respect

*It is not a disgrace
to not reach the stars,
but it is a disgrace to have
no stars to reach for*

A good book is a source of great knowledge and wealth for many generations

Dream, dream, dream
Your dreams will transform into thoughts
Thoughts lead to honest work
Work will result in actions
And you will succeed

The higher the proportion of creative leaders in a nation, higher the potential of success of visions like "Developed India"

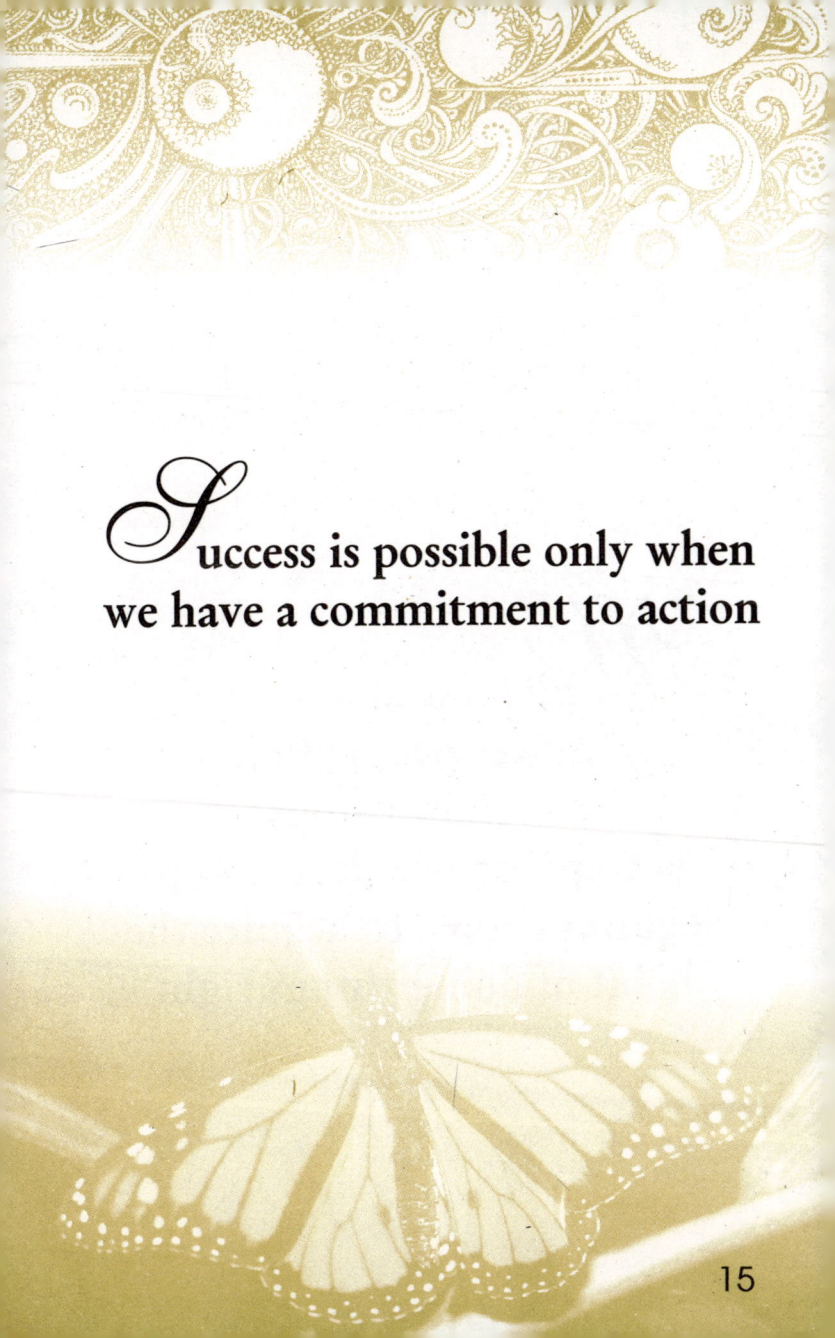

Success is possible only when we have a commitment to action

While moral leadership
requires people to do
the right things,
entrepreneurial leadership
requires people to acquire the
habit of doing things right

Connectivity is strength
Connectivity is wealth
Connectivity is progress

Perception of disability lies in the mind

When learning is purposeful,
creativity blossoms
When creativity blossoms
thinking emanates
When thinking emanates
knowledge is lit
When knowledge is lit
the nation progresses

With determined efforts you can always succeed against established beliefs

Always be ready to
walk the unexplored path

𝒜 great mind and a great heart go together

You will be remembered for creating a page in the history of the nation

The whole universe is friendly to us and conspires to give the best to those who dream and work

Enlightened citizenship has three components : education with value system, religion transforming into spiritual force, and creating economic prosperity through development

One cannot stop at thinking and asking questions. There is need to act to solve the problems and that requires hard work and perseverance

Creativity and imagination of the human mind would always be superior to any computer

Education is an endless journey through knowledge and enlightenment

Can we make an education system which will retain the smiles on the faces of our children?

It is through the process of innovation that knowledge is converted into wealth

Beautiful minds
are the source of creativity

Creativity is the foundation of human thinking and will always be at the highest end of the value chain

Learning gives creativity
Creativity leads to thinking
Thinking provides knowledge
Knowledge makes you great

Every mind is creative, every mind is inquisitive

The precious asset of a country is the skill, ingenuity and imagination of its people

Thinking is progress
Non-thinking is destruction
Thinking leads to action

Knowledge without action is useless and irrelevant
Knowledge with action brings prosperity

What was thought
impossible has happened
and what is thought possible
has not yet happened
but it certainly will happen

The education system has a tremendous responsibility to transform a child into a leader - the transformation from 'What can you do for me' to 'What can I do for you'

Conscience is a great ledger where our offences are booked and registered

The most important part of education is to imbibe among the students the spirit of 'we can do it'

*H*ard work and perseverance are beautiful angels who will reside on your shoulders

An ignited mind is the
most powerful resource
on the earth,
above the earth and
under the earth

$\mathcal{T}$he three key societal members who can make a difference are father, mother and teacher

*O*nce taught, children become conscience keepers

Education and values imparted in childhood are more important than the education received in college and university

In a society
we have to build
righteousness
among all its
constituents

The twenty-first century is about the management of all the knowledge and information we have generated and the value addition that we can bring to it

Science and spiritualism seek the same divine blessings for doing good for the people

Enlightened leadership is all about empowerment

In whatever field we work,
we have to remain in the
service of the common man
whose well-being is central to
all human knowledge
and endeavour

Our righteous toil is
our guiding light
If we work hard
we all can prosper
Nurture great thoughts
rise up in actions
May righteous methods
be our guide

Teachers themselves should be lifelong learners

A virtuous man alone can use the instrument of conscience

I believe there is no other profession in the world that is more important to society than that of a teacher

A candle loses nothing by lighting another candle

𝒞onscience is the divine light of the soul that burns within the chambers of our psychological heart

A teacher's life lights many lamps

What matters in this life more
than winning for ourselves,
is helping others win

A teacher has to create a lifelong autonomous learner

Teachers have a great mission to ignite the minds of the young

he convergence of science and technology with spirituality is touted to be the future for both science and technology, and spirituality

When a leader empowers the people, such leaders are created who can change the course of the nation itself

Coming into contact with a good book and possessing it is an everlasting enrichment of life

𝒢ive one hour a day exclusively for book reading and in a few years you will become a knowledge centre

Science is all about asking questions and finding the right answers through hard work and research into laws of nature

Music is a great communication and language can never be a barrier

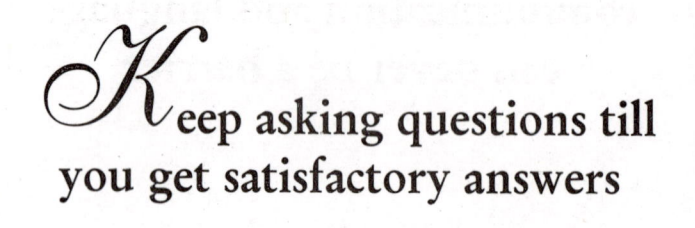

Keep asking questions till you get satisfactory answers

Authors act as conscience keepers of the society

Music and dance can be used as an instrument for ensuring global peace and act as a binding force

The crowning glory of a nation is its thinkers

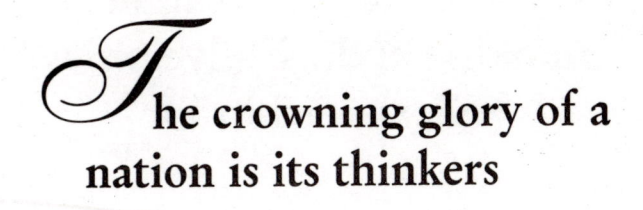

It is the privilege of authors that they can help mankind endure adversities and succeed in life

Learning needs freedom to think and freedom to imagine, and both have to be facilitated by the teacher

Music and dance elevate you to a different plane altogether and give you a breeze of happiness and peace

A combination of knowledge, enthusiasm and hard work of the youth is a great dynamic fire for transforming the nation

A nation is great because of the way its people think

If India is to become developed by 2020, it will do so only by riding on the shoulders of the young

Literature elevates the mind

The young population of India must have a big aim, small aim is a crime

All of us need to think and realise that the nation is greater than any one individual or organization

We should all create a nation that is one of the best places to live in on this earth and which brings smiles to a billion faces

Strength respects strength

Only when each and every citizen has been empowered so that he can lead a fulfilled life with dignity, will there be national peace and prosperity

All of us have to work hard and do everything possible to make our behaviour civilized to protect the rights of every individual

Repeating what we did before for several decades with more of the same may not be the way to proceed further

Encompassing the needs, rights and expectations of youth to the centrestage of development should be our priority

*N*ot only does the teacher provide knowledge, but the teacher also shapes the student's life with great dreams and aims

The role of the teacher is like the proverbial 'ladder'- it is used by everyone to climb up in life - but the ladder stays in its place

Science is the best boon
that God has bestowed
upon mankind

A good sign of a developed nation is that 'people who have' work hard to bridge the divide between themselves and
'those who have not'

From the emperor down
to the common man,
the cultivation of the righteous
life is the foundation for all

At the frontier,
there are no borders

We have a right and responsibility to leave a positive legacy to the posterity for which we all will be remembered

Technology is the non-linear tool available to humanity which can effect fundamental changes in the ground rules of economic competitiveness

Our sweat will transform Developing India into a Developed India

Transformation is an outcome of a farsighted vision, innovative mind and guiding spirit

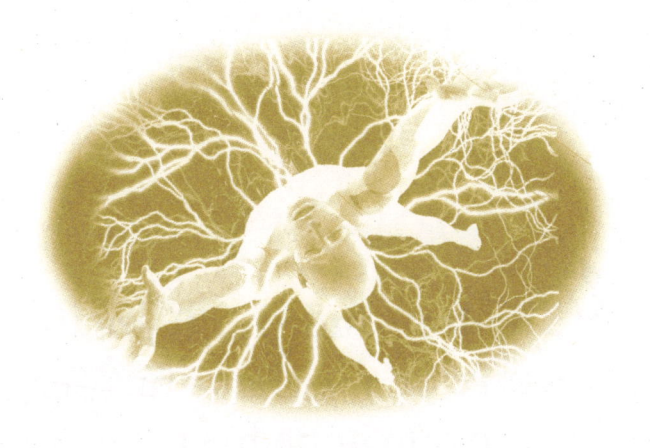

Art helps to bring out the beauty of life in its noblest forms, imparting meaning and depth to human existence, justifying and vindicating the purpose for which life was evolved

Children and youth are the picture of a nation's future. They are our hope for tomorrow

The science that we work with today must have the innovativeness, foresight and the vision for it to be the centre of technology that we develop tomorrow

Focus of the education system should be to train students to become autonomous learners

*Enlightened spiritual
and scientific leaders
all converge towards giving
reverence to human life*

Science and
science pursuits
are borderless

Any country is as
good as its citizens;
their ethos, their values
and their character
will be reflected in
the country's make-up

Each one of us on this planet creates a page in human history irrespective of who he or she is. I realise my experience is a small dot in human history, but that dot has a life and light